WHY GOD PERMITS ACCIDENTS

I0807587

by Spiros Zodhiates, Th. D.

COVER DESIGN BY FLORENCE ANDERSON

PRINTED IN THE UNITED STATES OF AMERICA
SECOND PRINTING NOVEMBER 1986

ISBN 0-89957-537-4

12-89-2500

Why God Permits Accidents

AMG Publishers. Chattanooga, TN. 37422

Dedicated to

my beloved friend, DR. HEINZE-HORST DEICHMANN, whose philosophy is that accidents and misfortunes in the lives of others are opportunites for deeds of compassion in the Name of Christ.

Preface

Can we blame God for the accidents that we or others experience? Is it your attitude that by virtue of having escaped accidents you are thereby more favored of God than others who have not escaped? What is God's purpose in accidents, anyway? Why should He permit them at all?

Jesus Christ, God's spokesman in human form, discussed this problem with His disciples. I'm glad He did, otherwise we would still be guessing. His discussion of the problem is found in Luke 13:1-9. I strongly urge you to read this passage before reading the book. So that you may easily do so, we have printed it here for you in its entirety.

The subject of suffering resulting from

accidents and other causes has been one of the most perplexing for both the believer and the unbeliever. Little do we stop to realize that believers are not automatically exempt from suffering. Nor are unbelievers automatically sentenced to suffering, at least not in this world.

In this book you will read not only of God's general, common blessings to all, such as the air we breathe and the rain which sustains our life on earth, but also of His special blessings, such as salvation, which is individual in its nature and its appropriation.

As with blessings, so it is with sufferings, also. There are general, common sufferings, including accidents, from which believers are not *necessarily* exempt, although they may sometimes be spared from them. There are also, however, special sufferings which God brings upon individuals in retribution for individual sins. But these sufferings are not necessarily experienced to their fullest extent in this world. However, they will be inescapable in the next world, even as the particular blessings of the believer will be fully experienced there.

You will be less confused about the origin and purpose of accidents and suffering after reading this book. At least I wrote it with this goal in mind. My prayer is that I may succeed in your particular case. If so, please write and let me know.

—Spiros Zodhiates

CONTENTS

Part One

Tragedy in the Headlines

How Is God Involved?

An airliner carrying almost two hundred people crashes in the coastal waters off Florida. Ninety passengers die, an equal number are spared. Scanning the terrible headlines in the morning paper we cannot suppress the questions rising in our minds. Why do such tragic accidents occur? Does a mindless chance determine who shall die and who shall survive, or does divine Providence touch the lives of men?

In the Soviet Union a book was written that caused a furor around the world and brought cries of "treason" from the author's government. Alexander Solzhenitsyn had chronicled the grisly history of the Stalinist police methods that he witnessed in the labor camps of the "Gulag Archipelago," when thousands of his fellow Russians fell victim to their rulers' brutality. "Where is the justice of God?" men ask. "Why does He permit such cruelty by the powerful against the weak?"

The Bible does not ignore the question of why we suffer, why evil men kill innocent people, why wars ravage mankind, why some die suddenly in accidents while others are permitted to live in peace and die with dignity.

From Genesis to Revelation the Bible portrays lives that, whether saintly or sinful, experienced the joys and sufferings common to men everywhere. These men, and the generations of those who followed them, sought for an answer, or perhaps a formula, that would give meaning to their sufferings. Sometimes they sought Scripturally, and were led of the Spirit. At other times their own pride led them astray, or their pain drove them to the ultimate despair of railing against their God.

Thoughtless observers of the events of history have asserted that divine Providence is capricious, or that everything that transpires is the result of blind forces. Some have concluded grimly with the poet that man is "slave to fate, chance, kings, and desperate men."

Still others, seeking a system of justice to account for life's misfortunes, concluded that those who suffered were being punished for special or secret sins. "Who ever perished, being innocent?" asked Eliphaz of the guiltless Job (Job 4:7).

We are heirs to this accumulated "wisdom" of mankind. How often does it reflect the Biblical view of suffering? What solace can we offer those who ask sincerely, as did David, "Hath God forgotten to be gracious? hath he in anger shut up his tender mercies?" (Ps. 77:9). Can we affirm that in the midst of the mysteries that enshroud life there is the pervading presence of a living God?

If we believe, as Jesus clearly taught, that the sparrow does not fall without our Father's will and permission, that He has numbered the very hairs of our head, we must conclude that God is profoundly involved in the struggles of our lives. Remembering that "we have not an high priest that cannot be touched with the feeling of our infirmities; but was in all points tempted like as we are" (Heb. 4:15), we can look with confidence to the comfort and wisdom of His Word.

When the headlines horrify us, or a personal tragedy darkens our lives, we can turn in our confusion to an all-knowing God, who, the suffering Jeremiah tells us, "doth not afflict willingly nor grieve the children of men" (Lam. 3:33). Instead, the testimony of the people of God was that "In all their affliction he was afflicted, . . . and in his love and in his pity he redeemed them" (Isa. 63:9). This is the compassionate God we serve. Let us keep this in mind as we face the questions that arise with suffering, and as we test the spirits of those who hasten to point out the reasons for our pain.

In Albert Camus' novel, *The Plague*, a priest stands with Dr. Rieux beside a dying child. While admitting the horror of the spectacle the priest says, rather lamely, "Perhaps we should love that which we cannot understand." The doctor replies grimly and with emotion, "No, Father. I have another idea of love. I shall refuse until death to love that creation in which children are tortured."

Such an attitude, while perhaps understandable, leads only to despair. We must refuse to engage ourselves in such ultimately barren answers to those questions that seem to defy solution. Like the Apostle Paul, "We are perplexed, but not in despair . . . cast down, but not destroyed" (II. Cor. 4:8, 9). "One who has never been bewildered," says Erich Fromm, "who has never looked upon life and his own existence as a phenomenon which requires solution and yet, paradoxically, for which the only answers are new questions, can hardly understand what religious experience is."

We are certainly not wrong in trying to understand the meaning of our experiences, particularly when they involve adversity or death. Men will inevitably ask honest questions in an effort to find meaning in their misery: Am I suffering for some special sin? Does God speak to us through suffering? Does He punish wrongdoing in this life as well as in the life to come? Are natural catastrophes a form of judgment? These do not lend themselves to easy answers. But let us examine the Biblical teaching on suffering, and measure against God's changeless Word the speculations and proposals of human reasoning. Let us keep in mind, too, the character and wisdom of Him with whom we have to do, "The high and lofty One that inhabiteth eternity, whose name is Holy" (Isa. 57:15).

God's Handwriting

He writes in characters too grand
For our short sight to understand;
We catch but broken strokes, and try
To fathom all the mystery
Of withered hopes, of death, of life,
The endless war, the useless strife—
But there, with larger, clearer sight,
We shall see this—His way was right.

—John Oxenham

from *Bees in Amber* American Tract Society

Jesus Responds to Some Bad News

An important passage of the New Testament that deals with the questions of suffering and providence is found in Luke 13:1-9. The discussion resulted from a public slaughter ordered by the Roman procurator, Pontius Pilate.

Pilate ruled Judea from A.D. 26 to 36, and his administration was marked by cruelty and many massacres. The one referred to by Luke had occurred in the Temple area during the Feast of Tabernacles. Pilate's henchmen, disguised as worshipers, had suddenly attacked and killed a group of Galileans, literally mingling their blood with that of their sacrifices.

This carnage was apparently in retaliation for a conspiracy that was brewing in the often seditious northern province of Galilee. Pilate had caused resentment throughout Jerusalem by confiscating Temple monies for the purpose of improving the cities' water supply, woefully inadequate at that time.

No doubt Pilate felt justified in so funding this project, but to his devout subjects this was a misuse of sacred funds and an intolerable affront. Responding with the impetuousness typical of him, Pilate acted to quell the embryonic rebellion. His slaughter not only violated the much-touted Roman rule of justice, but he was also probably acting outside his jurisdiction. These Galileans were actually subject to King Herod and should have been referred to him, as one day a shaken and subdued Pilate would refer another Galilean prisoner, Jesus of Nazareth. We know that, until that trial brought them together again, Pilate and Herod remained obdurate enemies, perhaps as a result of this rash and bloody action in the Temple.

The event may have just taken place when several men of Jerusalem interrupted Jesus' teaching to relate the shocking story. The Greek expression in Luke 13:1 translated "at that season" is *en autoo too kairoo. Kairos* (the nominative case) refers to opportunity, rather than simply "time." It is used in Matthew 13:30 as *kairos therismou,* "time of harvest," and in Mark 11:13, "time of figs." The literal translation of the Greek of Luke 13:1 would be, "And there came certain ones to announce to him at that particular time, or, as the opportunity arose, concerning the Galileans whose blood Pilate had mingled with their sacrifices."

These "reporters" seem to have been people who came to Jesus not to be taught by

Him but to seize an opportunity to confront Him with disturbing questions. They seemed less concerned about Pilate's atrocity than about ascertaining the guilt of his victims. That this was their real interest is evident from Jesus' reply in the form of a question: "Suppose ye that these Galileans were sinners above all the Galileans, because they suffered such things? I tell you, Nay . . ." (vv. 2, 3). Jesus, reading their hearts, rebuked their judgmental attitude and reminded them of another recent tragedy where eighteen men were killed by a falling tower at Siloam, possibly during the construction of Pilate's new water system. "Think ye that they were sinners above all men that dwelt in Jerusalem? I tell you, Nay . . ." (vv. 4, 5). Both of these calamities had stunned the city of Jerusalem. Such disastrous events raised questions then, as they do today, concerning God's judgments and man's responsibility.

However, the religious leaders of the day had available what seemed a plausible answer. Those who suffered in such ways were undoubtedly evil men, and the calamity was a direct visitation of God upon them. This is what the men of Jerusalem were implying and what they apparently wanted Jesus to confirm.

Instead, He quickly refuted that pernicious doctrine, as well as the tendency, universal among men, to judge rashly.

Jesus did not attempt to explain or interpret these terrible events—one an accident, the other an atrocity—but He did indicate to His inquirers what their attitudes should be: rather than judging the unfortunate victims of these tragedies, they should take warning and examine their own hearts. For, He declared emphatically, "Except ye repent, ye shall all likewise perish" (vv. 3, 5). Wishing to express His deep concern for their souls, Jesus repeated His admonition. These men had not recognized any connection between these recent visitations and the need in their own lives. Jesus was concerned that in the days in which God extended His grace they should find shelter under the panoply of His mercy.

Perhaps He looked ahead to the devastation that Rome would inflict on this city in the coming generation and longed to spare its citizens that suffering. Perhaps He thought of these men, this conversation, when only days later He grieved over the recalcitrance of His beloved city. "O Jerusalem, Jerusalem, which killest the prophets, and stonest them that are sent unto thee; how often would I have gathered thy children together, as a hen doth gather her brood under her wings, and ye would not!" (Luke 13:34).

His message to them had been clear: This tragedy must not lead you to judgment, or to complacency, but to repentance. Let us not repeat their mortal error by being so concerned with our own questions that we cannot hear His voice speaking through the storm of our lives.

Choose Thou For Me

I dare not choose my lot;
I would not if I might.
Choose Thou for me, my God;
So shall I walk aright.

The kingdom that I seek
Is Thine; so let the way
That leads to it be Thine,
Else surely I might stray.

Take Thou my cup, and it
With joy or sorrow fill;
As best may seem,
Choose Thou my good or ill.

Choose Thou for me my friends,
My sickness, or my health;

Choose Thou my cares for me,
My poverty, or wealth.

Not mine, not mine, the choice,
In things or great or small.
Be thou my Guide, my Strength,
My Wisdom, and my All!

—Horatius Bonar

Part Two

Suffering: An Accident of Chance?

The Ways of Providence

One of the greatest ships ever built was the famed Titanic. Although advertised worldwide as unsinkable, it hit an iceberg on its maiden voyage in April 1912 and sank, taking hundreds of passengers to the bottom of the sea.

G. Campbell Morgan, the great English preacher, lamented the loss of a personal friend who went down with the ocean liner. Preaching at Wesminster Chapel in London on "The Loss of the Titanic," he made an observation that every thinking man ought to consider:

> There is a Providence watching over the affairs of men, controlling even the choices that are made in human freedom, not to immediate results, but to ultimate and final issues. I say there are quantities of facts and qualities, of which we are ignorant, all of which must be taken into account if we are to have an accurate interpretation of providential dealings.

Morgan was addressing himself to the

question that must have stirred many hearts that April day: Where does the providence of God enter into such a catastrophe as this? Was it "providential" that some who bought tickets for this voyage never boarded ship; and did God withhold His providence from the others who sailed and perished? How are we to understand God's providence?

We do not find the term itself applied to God in the Scriptures. But the definition of "providence"—that God is continually at work preserving and governing the world—is clearly a Biblical truth. "The Lord hath prepared his throne in the heavens; and his kingdom ruleth over all" (Ps. 103:19). Few would argue the point that God is Master of His universe, "upholding all things by the word of his power" (Heb. 1:3), but may misunderstand how God's providence affects them in their daily lives.

Throughout the Gospels we find that Jesus' doctrine of providence was total, presenting a negative as well as a positive aspect. The Lord taught that our Heavenly Father cares for all; that the very hairs of our head are numbered. But He also on occasion ascribed some unhappy circumstances to God's account; the blind man, we are told in John 9:3, was handicapped that "the power of God might be manifest in him"; Pilate's authority to harm Jesus was given him "from above" (John 19:11).

This does not often correspond with our one-sided understanding of God's providence. We commonly think of the many times He has protected us from evil and harm, perhaps in an exceptional manner, and we call these the providences of God. We forget that an accident, an illness, or any other grief is also within God's providence, however undesirable the experience may be.

At other times we mistakenly assume that an act of providence is God's protection for good people like us. That false coin has another side, equally spurious, which is that all who suffer must be evil, since God has not delivered them!

But such a doctrine is quickly shattered against the hard facts of life. We often see the "good" suffer and the "wicked" escape. During that same week in which the Florida plane crash took so many lives, a church bus traveling a Texas highway met with a violent accident. Eighteen young Christians en route to a youth retreat were killed. So Pilate's massacre in the Temple and the debris falling at Siloam may very well have destroyed both saints and scoundrels.

We must therefore reject the notion that the sufferer has always incurred Heaven's displeasure, while those who prosper are necessarily the objects of God's special providence. We shall do well to remember the words of the Lord Jesus to His disciples in John 16:33, "In the world ye shall have tribulation." He had just previously said to these close friends in that same verse, "In me ye . . . have peace." But the peace of God residing in their hearts would not guarantee freedom from tribulation in the world.

The "Act of God," So Called

The insidious idea behind the designation "Act of God" is one that Jesus would surely have resisted. He reminded His listeners often of God's providential goodness, "causing his rain to fall on the just and the unjust" (Matt. 5:45), and would hardly have countenanced the labeling of calamities as special acts of God.

The collapse of the tower at Siloam might today have been put in that category, since it was an unforeseeable accident. Lawyers and journalists frequently use the term "Act of

God'' when discussing such events. The term has been defined as "a result of natural forces, unexpected and not preventable by human foresight." A judgment by the courts that an accident was an Act of God frees one from liability for any resulting damage. In other words, it's not your fault, it's God's!

This is sorry logic when carried into our daily lives. How can we ascribe to God circumstances we would prevent if we could, and dismiss the unearned benefits that accrue to us daily—the bounty we could never secure by any amount of foresight? Are these not equally Acts of God?

We are strange people, singling out as God's actions the misfortunes we cannot explain and forgetting those myriad mysteries that sustain and bless our lives: the balances of nature, the regularity of the seasons, the wonder of birth and growth. All these are the Acts of God, as is every human life and every death.

The Jews reporting bad news from the Temple to Jesus clearly believed that, while Pilate perpetrated the crime, he was simply the messenger of God's judgment. Jesus did not say anything to contradict this view. If all events whatever are in God's sovereign disposal, and if not so much as a sparrow or a human hair perishes without His leave, we may be certain that the lives of men are more particularly under His providential care; that they are never sacrificed to any man's rage, or taken away by violence, without His sufferance. In this sense God is the Author and Disposer of all events, operative in all that comes to pass in the world, directing all things toward an appointed end. This is the meaning of God's providence.

We may not—cannot—always understand His ends. But, learning from the Lord Jesus, we can trust God in the hour of crucifixion, when the crowd of friends has thinned out and darkness overwhelms us. In the resurrection light all will be made clear. There is a life of fuller freedom beyond this present one, when the providential paths we trod will be seen with better eyes. "Then shall [we] know even as [also we are] known" (I Cor. 13:12). (See "Accidents and Providence," by Frederick C. Spurr, in the *Christian World Pulpit*, vol. 10, pp. 289-91, and vol. 81, p. 258.)

Part Three

Suffering: A Sign of Guilt?

Specific Sin and Specific Punishment

During the Second World War the courageous German pastor Martin Niemoller resisted the Nazis and as a result spent eight years in a concentration camp. Just before Christmas 1944 one of his daughters attempted to visit him in prison. On the pretext that she was too young, the Nazis refused her permission. Shortly thereafter the sixteen-year-old girl became gravely ill with diphtheria and died. Niemoller was informed of this by a heartless guard who said, "Ha, one of your children is dead." The pastor asked, "Would you have the grace to tell me which one?" He was finally permitted to talk to his wife on the phone. After their conversation Mrs. Niemoller, shattered by grief, returned to her room. On her desk she found a photo of her young daughter. Beneath the picture her son had written this verse from the Book of Job: "Hitherto shalt thou come, but no further" (Job 38:11). Mrs. Niemoller bowed before the mystery of life and death and wept. She would face living each day with an open wound, revolving her life around unanswerable questions.

Rare indeed is the person who would consider that Niemoller and his family were suffering for their sins. It is apparent instead that the suffering was a direct result of their righteousness. And yet the old notion, rampant in Jesus' day and common still in ours—that suffering is a sign of guilt—dies hard.

That there is a mystery concerning why God permits circumstances in which some suffer and die while others go unscathed we cannot deny. In their efforts to resolve the mystery some people have yielded to the temptation to associate grief with guilt. "You suffer; therefore you must have sinned."

In pagan cultures it is quite generally believed that suffering is a form of punishment. In ancient times, to be ill or diseased was evidence of being posessed by the devil. Sick people were sometimes subjected to terrible tortures in order that the evil might be driven from them.

Among the first-century Jews a belief that suffering was the consequence of sin was so prevalent that Jesus' disciples asked Him concerning the man born blind, "Master, who did sin, this man, or his parents, that he was born blind?" (John 9:2). The men of Jerusalem were reflecting this widely-held belief when they suggested to Jesus that the Galileans killed by Pilate suffered that fate because of some special sinfulness. But He rejected their assumption, as we have seen in Luke 13:2, 3. "Suppose ye that these Galileans were sinners above all the Galileans, because they suffered such things? I tell you, Nay. . . ." Instead He indicated that they themselves were in the same position as the victims: "Except ye repent, ye shall all likewise perish."

We must be careful to note that the Lord docs not deny that suffering in general is due to the existence of sin. What He repudiates is the idea that special suffering indicates special sin. Physical death, according to the Lord Jesus Christ, is not necessarily the consequence of specific sin, nor is suffering on this earth always a sign of God's displeasure. Suffering and death have been the lot of all men since Adam. The corruption that followed the Fall marred every facet of human life. In this sense all misery can be laid at the door of sin.

The Lord Jesus did recognize, tacitly at least, that the Galileans were punished as sinners, and that the calamity that befell them was a judgment. What kind of men they were is not stated—whether they loved their families, paid their taxes, were good neighbors—but sinners they certainly were, and they could not suffer more at the hands of God than their sin deserved, nor can any of us, so deep is our iniquity. Temporary afflictions at their worst do not come up to the measure of men's sins; therefore the best men alive cannot suffer more than is due their transgressions.

Perhaps those Galileans were wicked men, since they were seditious, turbulent, factious, but not more wicked than their brethren. Beyond any question they were sinners and suffered in that extraordinary manner as a result of sin. The same may be asserted of any one of us visited with afflictions, because all men are sinners, encountering justly whatever they suffer in this world by the direction or permission of Almighty God.

What conclusions, therefore, may we draw as we observe the calamities that befall men? Those who maintain that all who suffer or die violently are the objects of God's wrath are clearly wrong. Is it not true that afflicted persons have often been God's best beloved children? It is difficult to remember a friend of God who did not undergo suffering; Abraham, David, Jeremiah, Paul, all experienced deep periods of grief. There is evidence that the disciples all died violent deaths except for John, and his waning years were spent in loneliness and imprisonment. Sinners though all these were by nature, they had been reconciled to God in Christ, pardoned, sanctified, and were hopeful of a joyous resurrection.

Many times such good men are afflicted, not because God would punish, but because He would glorify them, test their faith, increase their virtues, and ultimately heighten their eternal rewards. Yet these purposes do not contradict the principle that all misery and pain, all trouble and anxiety, are related to sin, for it is sin that has brought forth suffering, death, and all the discomforts incident to mortality. In a sinless world, such sufferings would have no place.

If the Jews had regarded instances of calamitous visitation simply as evidence of the universal destroyer, sin, without indulging in comparisons or attempting to relate punishment to offense, the words of our Lord condemning their hasty judgment need never have been uttered. The error that Jesus condemned was not their belief that the victims were sinners, nor was it even their conviction that suffering is the consequence of sin. These principles had long been established in the memories of a people often punished by God for their sins as a nation. Their error was first of all in carrying these principles to the vicious conclusion that the unfortunate victims of the tower that fell on them in Siloam were "sinners above all men that dwelt in Jerusalem" (Luke 13:4), and secondly that in so judging their brethren they usurped the place of God.

In the instances in the Bible where God brings punishment on individuals, He specifies the sin which incurred that punishment. Miriam's leprosy was a penalty for her rebellion against Moses (Num. 12:1-10); David lost Bathsheba's child because he had Uriah murdered (II Sam. 12:1-14); the captivity of Israel and Judah was punishment for their years of idolatry (II Kings 17:13-20 and many other references). But other instances of suffering are recorded with no accusation of offense: Naomi's loss of her husband and sons, Job's accumulated disasters, Paul's thorn in the flesh. The Scripture convicts none of these of special sin, yet they suffered.

Lacking any clear, specific revelation, it is dangerous for us to speculate on the causes of our own suffering. Certainly we should not presume to know the reasons for a brother's misfortune. Concerning ourselves we might wisely apply Paul's policy, "I judge not mine own self" (I Cor. 4:3), and, regarding others, Jesus' explicit command, "Judge not" (Matt. 7:1).

Do Sinners Suffer More?

The person who narrowly escapes injury in a close call, or who suddenly enjoys unexpected good fortune, is often told half-jokingly that it must be because he "lives right." People seem to have an idea lurking in the back of their minds that the good prosper, while the evil suffer. Much in nature and some words of Scripture seem to bear this out. Poverty often overtakes the sluggard, sickness the profligate, and imprisonment the criminal. The Scriptures declare, "The way of transgressors is hard" (Prov. 13:15) and, more vividly, "Evil shall hunt the violent man to overthrow him" (Ps. 140:11).

We are all acquainted with men and women whose selfishness and greed cost them the love of family and friends and left them at last in despair, alone with their avarice. Generosity and concern for others would certainly have won these sad souls more happiness and true prosperity.

We would be foolish, however, to expect that an upright life will guarantee continuous peace and happiness. The Bible never teaches this. Nor does it imply that the wicked will invariably suffer here on earth. David confessed to having seen the wicked prosper, "spreading himself like a green bay tree" (Ps. 37:35) and the most cursory study of Scripture and history will prove that many righteous men have been grievously afflicted.

In spite of this evidence, the suspicion remains that sinners will suffer more than saints. People seem to draw comfort or security from finding in those who suffer the cause of their grief—a flaw, a misdeed—which brought about the calamity, as if thereby to ward off any impending disasters from their own self-righteous heads.

So, perhaps the men of Jerusalem felt: "The Galileans are all half-Gentile, rough, uncivilized, simple; upon any of them destruction might with justice come; but we, who live beneath the shadow of the Temple, who frequent its courts and observe its ordinances, are guiltless; we are holy in comparison with them. They came to the Temple to create trouble and to rebel against Pilate. . . . They in reality brought upon themselves Pilate's vengeance, but we who live quiet and peaceable lives may well esteem ourselves safe from the Roman sword." (See *The Pulpit*, vol. 68, pp. 9-15.)

But Jesus, after rebuking their self-serving assumption, reminded them of the recent accident at Siloam to show that no one is truly safe from the "outrageous fortune" that all flesh is heir to, and repeated His warning, like a solemn refrain, "Except ye repent, ye shall all likewise perish."

There were those present at His crucifixion, months later, who saw His terrible suffering as the final evidence of His guilt, and the vindication of their rejection of Him. Their preconceived idea of God's justice held no place for the possibility that God could allow the innocent to suffer. They overlooked the many wise and good among their ancestors who had suffered. They misunderstood their own prophet Isaiah, who had foretold in detail how the Messiah would be afflicted.

If the Lord Jesus, this best and noblest of our race, this peerless Son of God and man, died so brutally, surely we can understand that the deepest suffering may be consonant with the purest innocence.

The Twin Hazards of Self-Righteousness

Along a dusty Palestinian lane halts the figure of a tired, dirty young man. His eyes, smarting from the sun and sand of a long journey, rise to scan the rich fields and green vineyards that surround him, and rest finally on a spacious homestead crowning the hillside. Unknown to the young traveler, two pairs of eyes are also studying him. One pair, aged, eager, full of pity, sees in the bedraggled bag of bones a long-loved son, returning home. The other pair, scornful, indignant, and severe, sees a destitute and craven derelict, shamed by a life of debauchery.

The father and the brother in Jesus' well-known story of the Prodigal Son seem to illustrate the kinds of attitudes people may adopt concerning another's misfortune. The older brother displayed the same spirit as the Jerusalem gossips whom Jesus rebuked: judgmental, insensitive, and self-righteous. The father, on the other hand, acted to restore and comfort the sufferer.

The brother's action was illustrative of that human failing which overestimates one's own goodness and enlarges another's sin. Rather than seeing in another's suffering a lesson for his own life, the self-righteous person concentrates on the possible guilt that may have brought on a brother's disaster. Jesus was teaching in Luke 13 that such accidents and misfortunes should be considered providential invitations to repentance and should serve as a means of driving sufferers and survivors alike closer to God. But the prodigal's brother, like the men of Jerusalem, deprived himself of this profound means of grace. (See *The Jerusalem Bible*, Luke 13, Notes.)

We must be careful, when we see others suffer, that we do not magnify their guilt and comfort ourselves with thoughts of our comparative innocence. None of us is exempt from grief; all are deserving of punishment. Such afflictions can serve as warnings to us, calling us from carnal ways and leading us to repentance.

Besides robbing us of a valuable lesson, a self-righteous attitude also prevents us from being of service to others in their need. The angry brother could not find it in his heart to furnish a warm welcome. Perhaps he and the men in Luke 13 reasoned, "If God thought these men so sinful as to be worthy of punishment, why should I involve myself in helping them?" Having first condemned, they could not readily be compassionate. These men would have done better to hasten to the families of those who were killed, to comfort and help them in any way they could. Among these families there must have been little children left homeless, without care. Instead of badgering Jesus, these citizens of the city could have been engaged in acts of charity toward those who were victims of Pilate's cruelty.

Thus there are two hazards we risk when we rashly ascribe another's suffering to his guilt. One is that, in the pride and deceitfulness of our heart, which is forever tempting us to think of ourselves more highly than we ought, we will fail to examine our lives and find the message God has for us in our brother's pain; the other is that, having judged our brother guilty, we shall soon cease to sympathize with him in his sorrow. We shall become like the proud men denounced in Isaiah 65:5 who said, "Stand by thyself, come not near to me; for I am holier than thou." We shall build a barrier between ourselves and the brother who needs us, and sadder still, between ourselves and God.

Judgment: The Prerogative of a Perfect Judge

"The longer I live," said scholar Jeremiah Day, "the more faith I have in providence, and the less faith in my interpretation of providence."

Day seemed to understand that the designs of providence are vast and large, God's thoughts very deep, His judgments unsearchable, His ways past finding out. And without a special revelation, which none of us can presume to have, we cannot know the particular errand upon which God's judgment may come.

In spite of these evident truths, we frequently fall prey to the temptation to consider natural calamities God's judgments on a society's sins. We have all heard public speakers do this at some time or another. On one such occasion a Christian leader was denouncing the gross sins of our present day and used a recent disastrous flood as an example of God's punishment. Among his listeners was one who had lost several loved ones in the flood and knew virtually all the victims to have been earnest believers, active in the Lord's work. Naturally, the listener's interpretation of the meaning of that catastrophe was quite different from the speaker's.

Perhaps our proclivity toward this kind of reasoning could be tempered by a look at some Biblical instances of judgment. When, for example, in I Samuel 15:1-8 we read that King Saul destroyed the Amalekites root and branch at the express order of God's prophet, but graciously spared the neighboring Kenites, he was actually carrying out a judgment pronounced three hundred years earlier, when the Amalekites had made war against the tribes of the infant nation of Israel (Exod. 17:8-16, Deut. 25:17-19), but the Kenites had welcomed them. (I Sam. 15:6 is the only direct reference to this in Scripture.)

Similarly, the severe judgments that fell on the house of Eli (I Sam. 3:11-14; 4:10, 11) and on Saul himself (I Sam. 15:10, 11; 31:1-6) came not only during their lifetime but also in later years. No one could have discovered the actual reason for these calamities had not God chosen to reveal them as His penalties for earlier crimes.

The Jewish historian Josephus ascribed the destruction of Jerusalem in A.D. 70 to the judgment of God on the monstrous wickedness of his countrymen at that time. To the

Christians of later generations it seemed instead a direct result of the city's rejection of God's Messiah.

As in trying to ascertain the sins behind a national disaster, so also in our efforts to pinpoint the cause of personal suffering, we are in danger of usurping God's prerogative. If He has not designated any crime for which a given misfortune may be punishment, have we any business doing so, no matter how obvious we may feel the cause to be?

Shimei, son-in-law to King Saul and his loyal adherent, made this mistake in the accusation he brought against King David in II Samuel 16:7, 8: "Thou bloody man, . . ." he shouted at the embattled old king, "The Lord hath returned upon thee all the blood of the house of Saul, in whose stead thou hast reigned; and the Lord hath delivered the kingdom into the hand of Absalom thy son: and, behold, thou art taken in thy mischief, because thou art a bloody man."

Shimei looked upon David as a usurper whose reign denied the rightful succession to the throne. Observing that by a strange turn of providence David himself was supplanted by his own son Absalom, Shimei jumped to the conclusion that God had declared judgment from heaven against David. On the surface the conjecture seemed quite plausible, as such human reasoning often does, but we know from Scripture that there was no truth in it.

David had the best possible grounds for claiming title to the throne: God had decreed that he should be king. If Absalom's rebellion was indeed a punishment from God upon David, the true cause was certainly not what Shimei proposed.

This incident may teach us caution and a holy reluctance to censure persons under affliction or to presume knowledge of the purposes of God. His judgments are like the handwriting that appeared on the wall before the eyes of the terrified Belshazzar: they may indeed be missives of God's anger; still, they require a prophet to read and interpret the fullness of their meaning (Daniel 5:17-28). Lacking such guidance, it is absurd and impious to assume the prerogative of judgment which belongs to Omniscience alone. Otherwise we border on the kind of superstition practiced by the pagans of Paul's day who, observing a deadly viper attach itself to the apostle's hand, immediately assumed he was a murderer, but just as quickly declared him a god when they observed further that he did not die (Acts 28:3-6)!

We cannot attempt to pronounce accurately the cause of God's judgments, because as creatures we are unable to enter into the secrets of an almighty, all-knowing, and eternal God. At our best we are beings whose wisdom is limited at every turn, having neither all the evidence on which to confirm a judgment nor the authority to pronounce a verdict.

At the conclusion of the Civil War, when hatred and vindictiveness were rampant in the land, President Lincoln sought to stem the tide of judgment and reprisal. When Senator Sumner of Massachusetts pressed him to have Jefferson Davis summarily hanged, Lincoln twice repeated our Lord's admonition, "Judge not, that ye be not judged" (Matt. 7:1). Though he had vanquished Davis as an enemy, Lincoln refused to condemn him as a man. He chose to leave that final judgment to his Creator. It may be that Lincoln's compassion was deepened by a small devotional book that was found after his death to be one he had read and valued. One selection in it was taken from Hebrews 13:3, "Remember them that are in bonds, as bound with them; and them which suffer adversity, as being yourselves also in the body." A brief verse under it read:

With pity let my breast o'erflow
When I behold another's woe,
And bear a sympathizing part
Whene'er I meet a wounded heart.

—*Lincoln's Devotional*
Channel Press, Inc.

Part Four

Suffering and God's Universe Law

On Treating Men Unequally

"Do you think that these Galileans were worse sinners than all the other Galileans because they suffered this way? I tell you, No . . . ! Or those eighteen who died when the tower of Siloam fell on them—do you think they were more guilty than all the others living in Jerusalem? I tell you, No. . . ." (Luke 13:2-5, N.I.V.).

When Jesus asserted so emphatically that physical disaster, like physical advantage, was no indication that the bearer was worse or better than his fellow men, He was saying something quite in harmony with modern thought but in direct oppostion to the popular convictions of the ancient world.

Since the days of Job, devout men had puzzled over the apparent injustices providentially meted out to men. The wicked often prospered, while the righteous suffered. "Wherefore do the wicked live, become old, yea, are mighty in power?" asked the confounded patriarch. "Their houses are safe from fear, neither is the rod of God upon them" (Job 21:7, 9). And David admitted, "I was envious at the foolish, when I saw the prosperity of the wicked" (Ps 73:3).

In a futile effort to "vindicate the ways of God to men," some people have explained all suffering as punishment rendered to a deserving sinner. If the victim appeared to have been righteous, so much greater was his culpability, for he obviously was a hypocrite as well!

If such reasoning sounds foolish and shallow to us, we must consider the ease with which the modern mind sometimes accepts simplistic answers. How often today do men "explain" injustice in the world by declaring that God is not in control, that He has "abdicated," is "dead," unmerciful, or impotent! The mocking ditty in Archibald MacLiesh's "J.B." is illustrative of some contemporary reasoning:

> If God is God he is not good,
> If God is good he is not God.

When some startling calamity brings ruin and death to many and suffering to countless families, someone will inevitably exclaim that providence is unfair or powerless. But the modern position is as bankrupt as the ancient one.

We would not deny that many times the best of men are permitted to fall sacrifice to the rage and violence of the worst of sinners. Hebrews 11:37, 38 recounts the suffering and slaughter inflicted on the saints, and declares that the "world was not worthy" of them, such was the esteem in which God held them. Why did He permit them to die so violently? Was it because, as the writer indicates, they were too noble for the present evil world? Or was it because their deaths would accomplish some high purpose in the plan of God? The Scripture does not say. We are told only that their deaths, far from being the result of God's displeasure, were a sign of His honor.

We know that afflictions and sudden disasters also come upon wicked men. At times this serves to rid the world of their evil influence; at other times it may drive them to repentance. Suffering may lead a man to God as pain leads him to a doctor. Still other men God may have given up as reprobate: no amount of grief or affliction will lead them to Him. He allows them to continue in their sin, and they eventually accumulate to themselves an eternal destruction.

Immediately after calling upon the men of Jerusalem to let the recent disasters lead them to repentance, Jesus told a significant story about a barren fruit tree. The parable in Luke 13:6-9 clearly illustrates God's patience and man's responsibility. When, after three years of cultivation, a certain fig tree produced no fruit, the owner was disposed to cut it down and replace it with another. In a land where fertile soil and water were at a premium, it was considered wasteful to allow an unproductive tree to cumber the ground. Jesus' listeners would have understood the owner's feeling. However, the vinedresser interceded for the tree, promising to fertilize and cultivate it, "and if it bear fruit thenceforth well; but if not thou shalt cut it down."

God's patience and longsuffering will not defer judgment forever. He uses both the sun and shadow of men's lives to bring them to Himself, but the responsibility to repent and to bear the fruit of faith belongs to men. "To whom much is given, of him is much required," Jesus said on another occasion (Luke 12:48). The one who fails to respond, and callously rejects God's calls to repentance, will suffer an eternal punishment all the more severe.

Conversely, while faith in God carries with it no guarantee of comfort in this world, it does carry great "recompense of reward" in the only world that really matters (Heb. 10:35).

Causes and the First Cause

A professor of theology at a Christian college began each school year by chalking on the board a simple rhyme that expressed his attitude toward life's contingencies:

In the center of the circle
Of the will of God I stand;
There can be no second causes,
All must come from His dear hand.

All of us must resolve in our minds, as this professor obviously did, a fundamental question: Is God responsible, directly or indirectly, for all the happenings in life? If we believe in only one God, we must necessarily conclude that He is the sole Master of creation. The belief that there is one God who rules the universe is called theism. It is the doctrine that God, who created the world, is also the One who sustains it and is ultimately responsible for all that takes place.

This is not to make God responsible for evil, or to ignore the role of Satan as "the prince of the power of the air, the spirit that now worketh in the children of disobedience"

(Eph. 2:2); but to say that God rules and overrules, as in the case of Joseph, who said to his brethren who had sold him into slavery in Egypt, "Ye thought evil against me; but God meant it unto good, to bring to pass, as it is this day, to save much people alive" (Gen. 50:20). And Psalm 76:10 tells us, "Surely the wrath of man shall praise thee: the remainder of wrath shalt thou restrain," so that God is always in control. Most conclusive of all, I John 3:8 declares, "For this purpose the Son of God was manifested, that he might destroy the works of the devil."

As for the reason God permits evil to continue to exist in this world, we can gain some insight from Judges 2:19-23, which says that, when Israel refused to drive out the Canaanites as God had commanded, and instead dwelt among them, followed their abominable customs, and worshipped their idols, God said He would no longer drive out the heathen nations before them, but would leave them as a test—to prove the Israelites, whether they would follow the Lord or not.

And that may be precisely why evil is permitted to exist today—as a test to see whether we will follow the straight and narrow way "which leadeth unto life" (Matt. 7:14), that is,

His way of salvation through faith in Christ and His atoning death, and obedience to Him as Lord of our lives.

Another system that has also been propounded is called deism, which is the belief that God, having created the world, has now retired from business and left things to look after themselves. According to the deist, the circumstances of life are the result of chance happenings.

Equally misleading is the philosophy called dualism, the idea that God and the devil are engaged in an eternal conflict. The dualist attributes all evil things to the devil and all good things to God.

The Bible makes it clear, however, that all things in the universe are the expression of one central life and power: there is but one God and He is ceaselessly at work in His universe. "My Father worketh hitherto, and I work" (John 5:17). It is the specific Christian teaching that God works in the world of His children as their Father: that is, that He directs men toward good and wise ends. We have the alternative choices of believing in such a God, or ascribing everything, our own lives included, to results of chance occurrence.

Can anyone really believe in "blind

chance"? We know that the universe is an orderly whole. Law reigns supreme. It can be trusted. If it were not for the trustworthiness of the physical laws, we could never have landed on the moon or probed the far reaches of space. The rising and setting of the sun, the ebb and flow of the tides, the procession of the seasons, the birth and death of worlds, even the seasonal rise and fall of the sap in the trees, proclaim a reign of order. And order never yet arose from chaos and never will.

Another element that mitigates against blind chance as the ultimate cause is that the balance of all things is heavily on the side of good, even as we regard good (though we are not always the best judges of what "good" is). If we knew all that is involved in God's universe, we might not speak of the balance of good against evil, but would see all things as good, being directed by God.

Regarding the laws of nature, we see that the world is not what some cynics would have us believe—a vast arena red with the blood of the vanquished in the eternal fight. It is, on the whole, a rich and fruitful place, in which life, growth, and harmony flourish. Those who malign the natural order as "cruel" exhibit little ambition to leave it, though they can find no room for its Maker in mind or heart. Proclaiming the world full of outrage, they continue to relish it and would do anything to lengthen their lives.

On a personal level we ought to realize that no misfortune or disaster happens but by God's direction or permission. Even things happening through second causes—the collapse of a building, the sword of an enemy—are subject to the First Cause, which is God. And, when He directs or permits second causes to afflict any man, He has a purpose in the affliction. It is never a matter of caprice.

The truth of the matter is that we can never fully explain those accidental deaths under fallen towers or in mangled airplanes, even when we locate the immediate cause of the tragedy—a structural defect, a human error. These are only second causes, certainly as subject to God's rule as anything else that takes place on the face of the earth.

It is good to observe the attitude of the Lord Jesus toward the whole scheme of things. He saw the Father in all, even in the fall of the sparrow—and the sparrow does fall. On a spring day, amid the beauties of the Galilean landscape, He proclaimed this truth of God's care over all things. It is easy, you may say, to preach like that in the spring of the year, when nature allures by her virginal beauty, and hopes rise with the fragrant fields. But there came another spring day when that same preacher hung impaled upon a cross, slowly dying. What then did He think of the providence of God? When the horror of darkness had passed, He breathed out the trusting words, "Father, into thy hands I commend my spirit" (Luke 23:46).

Brought to that cross by hate, malignity, injustice, and unchained human passion, He refused to indict the natural order. To the end He believed in the goodness of God. And have not time and the results of that Good Friday, vindicated His assurance?

Laws, Natural and Spiritual

The means by which God governs is the means of ordered law. In this sense, natural law is the expression of God's providence. The regularity of nature persuades us that we are not governed by capricious forces but by definite laws administered by a sovereign God. Caprice results in disorder, the negation of government. But it is important to observe that the laws of God by which He governs are not separate from Him. This does not mean that God is synonymous with natural law, or that we pantheistically confuse nature with God. Rather, we understand that God is the divine Person, the extension of whose will is government by law. This law does not have a separate self-existence. Law is mind and will at work in orderly sequence. The laws of nature are the expression of the will of God. God works within the world order in a living way. All laws express the purpose of someone. The laws of the United States, for instance, express the will of the Congress, which in turn expresses the will of the people. And so the laws of nature express the purpose of God.

For the sake of convenience we may say that the world has two levels: a higher and a lower, a permanent and a temporary, a spiritual and a material. Man belongs at once to both orders, and he is subject to the laws of both. He belongs by his body to the material order. The same chemical elements that are in him are also in the material world around him: hence, he is subject to the operation of material forces such as gravitation, lightning, earthquakes, and such phenomena.

In the administration of these natural laws there is absolute impartiality. The sun is completely impartial concerning whom it shines on, and the rain on whom it falls. Nature plays no favorites. A saint and a scoundrel, unable to swim and adventuring into water beyond their depth, will assuredly be drowned unless outside aid rescues them. No angel hand will reach out to save the saint or sink the scoundrel. Both will die if they fall within the grip of a natural law that neither wit nor strength can overcome. What we call "accidents" are due in every case to disobedience, deliberate or unknowing, of some natural law. Ignorance does not save us. The child who is drowned under the eyes of helpless spectators is not attacked by some ferocious monster called "law" and cruelly deprived of life. The same water that sinks him will float him—if he knows how to use it properly.

The tower of Siloam killed the workmen, not because of any mysterious fate, but solely because of the bad materials or the bad workmanship in its construction. A tower built in a proper manner with good materials and on a proper foundation would not have fallen. But where the law is violated the results may be "bad" in the experience of the victims. There is neither fate nor design in what we call accidents. It is true, however, that the harsh effects of the law may tempt us to be bitter and resentful. But the law itself is good and right, and in our better moments we acknowledge this.

Man also belongs to a second order—the spiritual. We alone of God's creatures are able to make moral judgments on what happens to us and around us. We bear responsibility for our actions, and often suffer certain consequences when we defy spiritual laws. These natural results of vice are commonly known to all: disease accompanies promiscuity, delusions afflict the drunkard, obesity threatens the glutton. They cannot be considered special punishments from God, but they do tend to reflect the moral force governing the world and curtailing, to some extent, the growth of evil.

Even as the physical order has its own laws, so does the spiritual order. Man belongs to the spiritual order because he was created in the image of God. To be a complete and happy person he must love God and his fellow human beings. When he fails to do so he ceases to be what God intended him to be and resembles the animal, fighting to obtain his desire. Herein we touch the heart of man's misery and confusion.

The materialist will explain that man is an

aggressive animal on whom a spiritual idealism is wasted. But the wounds man inflicts on his fellows are not the result of his belonging to the material order, but are caused by his refusal to live according to the spiritual order. The law of love is the law of man's life. When he disregards it, man acts as an animal.

But if man is left free to obey or to disobey the laws of life, how can we say that God is directing events?

Robert Browning surveyed creation with an insightful eye and concluded, "All's law and all's love." He meant that God's laws are the expression of His love, and obedience to them will work for our ultimate good. When the ultimate good is obscured by a very present adversity, we must keep two basic considerations in mind:

The first one is that God rarely employs exceptional methods in dealing with us. God has on some occasions intervened in the history of mankind and in the lives of individuals. He has broken forth in demonstrations of His power that compelled men to acknowledge His presence. But this is unusual. His method is historically the continuous exercise of law. The reason for this is plain enough. If God's presence and care were made known only in exceptional or miraculous ways, we should forever be in a state of uncertainty, and this would make progress precarious. God has chosen to follow His laws because He wants us to depend on them. Jesus performed many signs and wonders during the years of His ministry, but the daily needs of His small band of friends were met in the usual manner. We learn and develop best, not in the spectacular, but in the ordinary and routine ways of life. God has given us the freedom to obey or disobey His laws; but to aid us in the exercise of this freedom, He has created and acts within this universe of law.

A second consideration we must bear in mind is that God guides and instructs us through our experiences. All the happenings of our lives are grist for His mill and are employed to perfect our spirits and train us for the next phase of our human life. We learn through our failures, our sorrows, our disappointments, our bereavements. In those dark seasons when we suffer unmerited pain or hardship, God supplies grace to help us rise above our material misery and to glory in the royalty of our spirit. With tears raining down our cheeks we can liberate the sunshine that creates the rainbow.

The believer can sing with Habakkuk: "Although the fig tree shall not blossom, neither shall fruit be in the vines . . . the flock shall be cut off from the fold, and there shall be no herd in the stalls: yet I will rejoice in the Lord, I will joy in the God of my salvation" (Hab. 3:17, 18). Such a man is no prisoner of natural law; he has the freedom of the universe, and his liberty proclaims the triumph of the spiritual order.

Part Five

Suffering: An Instrument of Love

Prodded to Repentance

The same sun that warms and melts the snow will harden and dry the clay. So the providence of God will work with varying results in the lives of His offspring. It is the inclination of our hearts, rather than the circumstance itself, that drives us nearer to God or away from Him in times of adversity.

David testified, "Before I was afflicted I went astray: but now have I kept thy word" (Ps. 119:67). A later king, Zedekiah, when afflicted because of his evil ways, "stiffened his neck, and hardened his heart from turning unto the Lord God" (II Chron. 36:13).

The Lord does not desire the suffering or death of the afflicted sinner, but rather that he should be converted and live. "When thy judgments are in the earth," said Isaiah, "the inhabitants of the world will learn righteousness" (Isa. 26:9).

God sees into the hearts of all men and knows what effect His visitation will have upon the one under affliction. He may be mercifully marking him out for suffering, knowing that this will bring him to repentance. God also sees the hearts of others more hardened in their sins and may totally reject them as past cure, giving them up to their own lusts. Paul discusses this possibility in the first chapter of Romans, saying of the pagans that God "gave them over to a reprobate mind" (v. 28). In a very real sense, then, God may be indicating to the sufferer that He considers him not beyond hope, but capable of being prodded to repentance. Sorrow can then be a gateway—though a constricting one—to forgiveness and joy.

God also has as objects of His mercy the survivors who witness terrible tragedy but are themselves spared. No doubt there were those eye-witnesses to the events in Jerusalem who asked in awe, "Why did God allow me to escape?" When all are sinners, God may consider it sufficient to warn the rest by the destruction of the few. He spares the majority, not because they do not deserve punishment, but because such examples of the precariousness of life may cause some to seek God in genuine repentance. Eternal suffering, after all, is much more to be avoided than any earthly pain; and if the latter delivers us from the former, it is a welcome affliction.

When Jesus used the word "perish," *apoleisthe* (from *apolumi*), in Luke 13:5, He was speaking of an eternal loss as opposed to a temporal one. He wanted His hearers to take advantage of a temporal destruction by truly repenting, and thus avoid an eternal one.

Observe how Jesus stressed these words by saying, "I tell you." Notice that He chose for "tell" the word *legoo*, meaning, "I speak with intelligence," rather than *laleoo*, which would imply that He was merely repeating or quoting something. Jesus spoke here as the divine Son who had participated in the whole counsel of God. It is as if He were saying, "I, who have come from heaven with the express purpose of saving you from perishing, give you warning to repent because I know what will happen if you don't."

Let us consider for a moment just what Jesus meant by the term "repentance." There are some who think repentance consists of conviction of sin, of contrition for sin, of confession to a priest or another person, even perhaps of doing penance for sin—as though we could possibly pay in coin or pain for the guilt in our souls!

Repentance is not any of these, or all of them put together. Nor is it merely having some transient passions of grief for one's sins, nor forsaking the most gross crimes to which we may have been addicted. Repentance is not any outward act whatever. As sin begins in our minds, so does repentance. It is motivated by what the Greek word for "repent" actually means. *Metanoieite* is made up of the preposition *meta*, "after," and the word for "think," *noeite*. It is the after-thought, a complete change of mental direction. It is nothing less than the recovery of the spirit from its former folly into a right frame of mind or constitution. Our Lord says, "Except you change your minds," and by that he means turning around our nature, our spiritual direction.

That is why Jesus described the repenting prodigal as "coming to himself," and so being of another, more sound and sober mind than he was before. Thus, when anyone truly repents, his mind is quite changed from what it was before; its bent and inclination have turned from sin to God. In other words, the term repentance as used by Jesus means nothing less than conversion. It is more than just conviction of sin, because conviction is like the realization that you are sick: it is the first step. Conviction without the next step, repentance, may make you miserable but it will never bring you peace.

Furthermore, repentance is not simply

contrition. Contrition is being sorry for your sin, but the Apostle Paul indicated that while there is a "godly sorrow [that] worketh repentance to salvation," there is also a sorrow that "worketh death" (II Cor. 7:10). Most men in prison will express sorrow that they are behind bars, but many are simply sorry that they got caught and had to suffer. Even in hell there is weeping and gnashing of teeth, but that sorrow has not worked toward repentance.

One can go through all the experiences of conviction, confession, and contrition, but still not repent. Almighty God, tempering justice with mercy in His providences, would lead us to that "godly sorrow [that] worketh repentance," expecting of us that true change of heart and mind that causes forsaking of sin and turning wholly to Him. No priest's confessional or psychiatrist's couch can ever rid us of the sin that separates us from God. But repentance in the Biblical sense will flood the heart and soul with the peace Horatio G. Spafford knew when he wrote:

My sin—oh, the bliss of this glorious
thought—
My sin, not in part, but the whole,
Is nailed to the cross, and I bear it no more;
Praise the Lord, it is well with my soul!

Chastened by the Father

In the prosperous days of the reign of the second Jeroboam, when Israel, riddled with idolatry and rife with injustice, seemed nevertheless to be increasing in power, God called a young shepherd from the hills of Tekoa to pronounce judgment on the land.

Amos spoke of the moral obligations of God's chosen race and their dismal failure in upholding His Word. He thundered against oppression and ungodliness, and threatened disasters to come. God's disappointment was great: "You only have I known of all the families of the earth: therefore I will punish you for all your iniquities" (Amos 3:2). Their special relationship with Jehovah made all the more poignant their alienation from Him. "Can two walk together," asks the next verse, "except they be agreed?" If God was to continue to work through His children, calling them His own, then He must punish them. Other nations might sin and escape; not so Israel. Because they were God's own, He would chasten them.

This continues to be the pattern in the New Testament, as God disciples the young Church. Hebrews 12:6, 7 speaks to Christians:

"For whom the Lord loveth he chasteneth, and scourgeth every son whom he receiveth. If ye endure chastening, God dealeth with you as with sons; for what son is he whom the father chasteneth not?" Jesus Himself speaks through John in Revelation 3:19, "As many as I love, I rebuke and chasten." What a marvelous Father-son relationship exists between God and the believer! Not only do our needs and desires come from His hand, but also the discipline of a faithful Father. He corrects us "for our profit, that we might be partakers of his holiness" (Heb. 12:10).

Our afflictions, therefore, can be understood as the pledge of God's favor toward us, the assurance of His concern. He refines the gold and removes the dross through the crucible of affliction, deepening our fellowship with Him and at the same time providing for His beloved a "great recompense of reward" in the life to come (Heb. 10:35).

The Apostle Paul in his tumultuous life must have suffered almost every affliction known to man. He testified to beatings, robberies, shipwreck, sickness, imprisonment, weariness, pain, hunger and cold, besides "that which cometh upon me daily, the care of all the churches." (See II Cor. 11:23-28.)

Hardly a stranger to grief and adversity, he recognized the hand of God and gloried in them, writing to the Romans, "O the depth of the riches both of the wisdom and knowledge of God! how unsearchable are his judgments, and his ways past finding out!" (Rom. 11:33).

Discerned in the Spirit

Later in the same chapter of Luke's Gospel that we have been studying, the evangelist records a brief incident of miracle and mistake. The miracle was Jesus' Sabbath-day healing of a crippled woman; the mistake was the accusation by a synagogue official that Jesus had violated Sabbath laws. Although a life had been transformed and God had been glorified, the myopic official could see only that Jesus had not worked according to the rules. In spite of his religious learning, the man did not understand God's Word or purpose.

When the learned men of Jesus' time came to Him with perplexing questions, the Lord made this blunt response, "Ye do err, not knowing the scriptures, nor the power of God" (Matt. 22:29). They erred because, though intelligent and educated men, they could not spiritually discern the real problems of life and solutions that exist for them.

Paul tells us that the spiritual man discerns all things. The natural man does not have this advantage because he cannot see the spiritual reality that exists all around and within us. He has a distorted view of the world, much as the insect, because of its own limitations, has a distorted view of the garden in which it crawls. How can one help being confused and perplexed if one is ignorant of God's great plan, and of the most vital and abiding of life's values?

Scottish theologian James Stewart wrote recently, "What a lost and crazy world it is, with its strange mingling of technological affluence and achievement on the one hand and spiritual impoverishment and famine on the other. . . ! But a Christian, looking out on the darkened scene, retains unshadowed confidence, because he knows there is another factor in the field and a greater Will constantly and unwearyingly at work: the immense pressure of a transcendent penetrating energy that fills the universe and every detail of creation." (James S. Stewart, *River of Life*, Hodder and Stoughton, London.)

Unbelievers are often confounded by the trust of the spiritual man. They may consider him naive, and mock his faith. Job's wife, having seen her husband fall from the pinnacle of success to grief and ignominy, enjoined him as he sat abandoned in the ashes to "curse God, and die" (Job 2:9). But Job's faith reflected a spirit fully committed to God's goodness: "Though he slay me, yet will I trust in him" (Job 13:15).

A child learns to walk and climb through many a tumble, and to behave through many a correction, because it is the nature of a child to learn. So our Christian growth will depend largely on the spirit in which we accept our corrections and adversities. We may let them sour or save us. Avoid them we cannot; transform them we can and must, if we are to live full and godly lives.

Through storm or sunshine we can put our confidence in God. We have, each of us, sufficient experience of the goodness of God and the benefit of His laws to sustain us when some calamity or reversal clouds the life and threatens to embitter the soul. We summon our past experiences and build upon them a new confidence. That is what the Lord Jesus did in His dark hour. "Into thy hands. . . ." (Luke 23:46). And because they are the hands of the Father, we are secure in committing ourselves to them.

In this life, complete light and vindication may not come. But for us, as it was first for our Lord, there will come a resurrection dawning when the sorrows and suffering of our Calvaries will forever fade in that bright light that the poet called "the white radiance of eternity."

Be still, my soul: the Lord is on thy side;
Bear patiently the cross of grief or pain;
Leave to thy God to order and provide;
In every change He faithful will remain.
Be still, my soul: thy best, thy heavenly
    Friend
Through thorny ways leads to a joyful
    end.

Be still, my soul: thy God doth under-
    take
To guide the future as He has the past.
Thy hope, thy confidence let nothing
    shake;
All now mysterious shall be bright at
    last.

—Katherina von Schlegel

Part Six

Joy in the Morning

Inexorable Justice, Unfailing Mercy

In order to understand fully the incident we find in the 13th chapter of Luke, we must go back to the latter half of the chapter that precedes it.

Our Lord had spoken to His disciples of how suddenly judgment sometimes falls upon men, and had pointed out that, while its culmination may seem catastrophic, the deeds that led to the judgment may have been building up for a long time.

In answer to a question posed by Peter in Luke 12:41, our Lord went on to say that, though judgment appears at times to be suspended, it always comes: the Master returns to take account of His servants' dealings. To this He added that, while judgment is very severe and always thorough, it is also discerning and equitable. The servant who neglected his lord's orders was more severely dealt with than the servant who failed in his duties through ignorance (Luke 12:42-48).

Then, in Luke 12:54-59, our Lord contrasted the shrewdness with which men can read the face of the sky and predict the weather with their obtuseness in the face of spiritual signs. And how menacing such stupidity is, seeing that judgment is inexorable, exacting the uttermost penalty, the very last mite!

If Jesus' words concerning judgment sound harsh to our minds, it may be because we humans have become conditioned to tolerating an enormous degree of sin but cannot endure suffering. We will go to any lengths to avoid pain, assaulting the gates of heaven and hell seeking relief. But it is evil that God cannot tolerate; sin is an abomination unto Him.

On the other hand, unpleasant as it may be for us to accept, God has permitted suffering and employed it for the perfecting of His children since the days of the patriarchs. God allowed His only Son, perfect and sinless though He was, to suffer immeasurably; but when out of love for us Jesus bore men's ancient and future sins, the sun darkened and the earth convulsed in abhorrence of the terrible event. Let us never underestimate God's loathing of sin, or the certainty and severity of His judgment upon it.

Jesus' parable of the barren fig tree was given as a reminder to all that God has not overlooked their offenses. Doom hangs over unrepentant sinners, although God in His mercy may defer it while He extends His grace.

The great Church father, John Chrysostom, in his third homily on the story of the rich man and Lazarus, has a beautiful passage concerning the wisdom of God in bringing judgment on some but not all. He says:

> But why, some say, are some punished here and others there (in the world to come) and are not all punished down here? For what reason? Because if this occurred, that is to say if all were punished down here, all of us would perish because all deserve punishment. Again, if no one was punished here, most of us would become careless and many would say there is no divine providence. This is why God punishes some down here, and some He does not punish. He punishes some, curtailing their evil . . . or altogether delivering them, and this makes sinners wiser as a result of their punishment. Others He does not punish so that if they examine themselves they would repent and they would be ashamed in view of the longsuffering of God, so that they may deliver themselves from judgment. (See *Works of John Chrysostom,* vol. 1. Athens: O Logos Publishers, 1967, p. 80. Translated by the author.)

God can wait. His is no human impatience, pressing things prematurely to an end. His grace holds back the arm of justice. He wills not that sinners perish but that all should turn and live. Yet His patience is not indifference. He is gracious but He is also righteous; His patience cannot make void the demands of His holiness. Although He is loving and compassionate, He cannot be mocked. To those who will be won by His love, He is love; to those who will walk in His light, He is light; but to those on whom both light and love are lost, He will be a consuming fire.

Afflicted, But Affirmed

In the days of His flesh Jesus knew by experience many of the trials and heartaches that afflict all men. The eldest son in a large family, He must have known the pain of separation when He left His home to begin the life of a traveling teacher, where He would have no certain place to lay His head, no family waiting at the end of the day, and where all roads would lead finally to a Roman execution.

On two occasions in the Gospels we find Jesus suffering the sudden loss of a close friend. John 11 relates how, in the household of Mary and Martha, a brother died after a severe illness. This home in Bethany had been the one refuge which had offered Jesus solace and simple friendship, where He had often retreated from the hassle and conflict of Jerusalem. The evangelist tells us that, as Jesus approached the crowded graveside of His young friend Lazarus, He wept openly. The fact that Jesus knew He could—and in this case would—return the dead to life did not relieve Him of the grief He felt for the suffering family, for the perishing condition of mankind, and for the countless times this sad scene would be repeated with no hope of a miracle.

On another day during Jesus' ministry the news was hurriedly brought to Him that His cousin, John the Baptist, long a prisoner of King Herod, had been suddenly and brutally beheaded. Jesus' deity did not shield Him from the shock and horror of that report, nor from the loss He must have felt of one who understood Him and His mission so specially. Matthew tells us that, after hearing the report Jesus departed by ship "into a desert place apart" (Matt. 14:13), there perhaps to pray and wrestle with a purpose that could allow Him to restore the villager Lazarus, but not the prophet John.

Could not Jesus have understood the

despair of the heart burdened with intense grief, questioning a life riddled with incongruities, pressed out of measure by what Camus called "the essential absurdity of life"? We do not walk an untrodden path. Cannot He, who was not ashamed to call us brethren, share in our darkest hour of suffering and shattered hopes? "In all their affliction he was afflicted, and the Angel of his presence saved them: in his love and in his pity he redeemed them; and he bare them, and carried them all the days of old" (Isa. 63:9). What a picture of a Savior who shares the experiences and bears the burdens of those He has redeemed! For the fellowship of His suffering He offers the power of His resurrection; all things, even the enigma that lies at the heart of our searing pain, are redeemed in His masterful hands.

The Bible throughout is ruthlessly faithful to the reality we experience. It nevers paints rosy pictures or offers simple solutions, or promises untroubled days. It offers instead an Advocate—the Spirit who stands with and within us, a Savior who shares the sorrows and triumphs of our lives, a Father who guides us and provides.

If we sometimes do not see His provisions in their full purpose, it is because our perspective is poor: we do not look from the center. The finite position from which we observe eternal acts distorts our perception. If we could perceive accurately, we would see that even our afflictions are mercies in disguise; the grace of God is subtly doing its perfect work. For all who must suffer pain or anguish there is a Comforter and the promise of His providence at last: "In his favor is life: weeping may endure for a night, but joy cometh in the morning" (Psalm 30:5).

I

INDEX OF SUBJECTS

II

INDEX OF ILLUSTRATIONS

III

INDEX OF ENGLISH WORDS

IV

INDEX OF GREEK WORDS